MORE THAN A
MIRACLE

WHAT IT TAKES TO GROW
AS A CHRISTIAN

JAMES A. SCUDDER

It Takes More Than a Miracle to Make a Christian Grow

ISBN: 978-0-9679145-3-4

24126 North Quentin Road
Lake Zurich, IL 60047
800-784-7223
ingrace.us

To Christians everywhere
as they grow in Christ.

Table of Contents

-1-

THE SECRET TO SPIRITUAL SUCCESS

---

*Either believe God to the hilt or else
don't believe Him at all.*
~C.H. Spurgeon~

When Pablo Casals reached 95, a young reporter threw him a question: "Mr. Casals, you are 95 and the greatest cellist that ever lived. Why do you still practice six hours a day?"

Mr. Casals answered, "Because I think I'm making progress."[1]

Many people wish there was a single secret to success in the Christian life. Maybe they think there is a special prayer they pray or a spiritual wonder-drug that causes instant growth in Christ. And yet, as Pablo Casals felt at 95 that his skill at the cello could still use some practice, so it is in the spiritual realm. It takes day-by-day, even moment-by-moment effort. But the result is maturity in Christ and that should be the goal of every Christian.

It is said that in the course of their conversation at a dinner party, Albert Einstein's young neighbor asked the white-haired scientist, "What are you actually by profession?"

"I devote myself to the study of physics," Einstein replied. The girl looked at him in astonishment. "You mean to say you study physics at your age? I finished mine a year ago."[2]

Just as Albert Einstein couldn't possibly learn all there was to learn about physics, neither can any Christian fully comprehend the wonders in the Word of God. But we can try, and in trying, we can learn what it means to walk with Jesus Christ. We can learn to have a relationship with Him that will surpass any relationship we have on this earth. This new fellowship will help us to be better siblings, spouses, and friends to all those around us. And it will fill a deep void in our lives, a spiritual vacuum that we may never have realized existed before we trusted Christ.

Over 2,000 years ago, Jesus Christ walked among men. He taught His disciples, His followers, and the crowds that mobbed Him. One of the ways that He taught was by using parables. A simple definition of a parable is a story that has a deeper, heavenly meaning. One parable that contains a lot of meaning for Christian growth is found in Mark 4:1–9.

And he began again to teach by the sea side: and there was gathered unto him a great multitude, so that he entered into a ship, and sat in the sea; and the whole multitude was by the sea on the land. And he taught them many things by parables, and said unto them in his doctrine, Hearken; Behold, there went out a sower to sow: And it came to pass, as he sowed, some fell by the way side, and the fowls of the air came and devoured it up. And some fell on stony ground, where it had not much earth; and immediately it sprang up, because it had no depth of earth: But when the sun was up, it was scorched; and because it had no root, it withered away. And some fell among thorns, and the thorns grew up, and choked it, and it yielded no fruit. And other fell on good ground, and did yield fruit that sprang up and increased; and brought forth, some thirty, and some sixty, and some an hundred. And he said unto them, He that hath ears to hear, let him hear.

If you plant eggplant, you aren't gonna get eggs!
Now, as He began to teach, the people could quickly identify with what He was saying. Farming was the principal means of people's livelihood in that day, and so it must have come as no surprise to the disciples that He would use such an illustration.

In your own mind, picture the farmer with a seed bag over his shoulder, walking (no John Deere tractors in those days!) in the fields sowing his precious seeds. These seeds probably had been taken from last year's crops and carefully stored so that no mildew or mold would ruin them. The seeds were the farmer's livelihood and were precious to him. But the day would come when he would begin to put those seeds into the already prepared ground. Whatever he planted, he expected to see grow. In other words, if he planted eggplant, he didn't expect to reap eggs! So it is in our lives. The principles of sowing and reaping hold true in every area.

A modern-day farmer was trying to teach his bad-tempered son how to control his bursts of anger. He told his son, "Each time you lose your temper and blow up, I'm going to put a nail in the gate. When you do something good, I'm going to take a nail out."

After a while, the boy saw that many nails littered the gate. He finally determined that he was going to stop getting mad and learn to control his temper. Soon, he noticed that there were fewer nails in the fence. Every time he did something good, his father took out more nails.

Finally, the boy had all the nails removed from the gate. His father came to him and said, "Son, I'm proud of you, but I want you to remember something. I'm glad all the nails are gone, but the scars from those nails are still in that post. God will forgive your bad temper, but you reap what you sow. When you see those scars you will be reminded of the lesson you have learned."

Just as the scars remained on the fence when the nails were removed, so the consequences of sin remain in the Christian's life long after the sin has been forgiven.

It is important then that we sow good seeds in our lives. Some of these "seeds" are attending a Bible-believing church, reading the Bible regularly, and praying often. When these seeds are planted in the ready soil (in future chapters we will talk about how to make the soil of our lives ready to receive the Word of God), they are sure to produce wonderful results.

We are also capable of planting bad seeds in our lives. When we turn away from that which is good, when we feed our minds with dirty images from movies or television, when we start leaning on our own strength instead of the strength of the Lord, all these things will result in a harvest of uselessness for the cause of Christ.

Decide right now to take this sowing and reaping principle to heart. Take a moment and pray that you will allow only good seeds to be planted in the garden of your life. Pray that you will resist the bad seeds so that when it comes time for harvest, you will have matured in your Christian life, walking closer than ever to your Savior.

Pray this prayer: Lord, I understand that what I sow in the soil of my life, I will reap. I pray that I will only sow wholesome things so that I may reap a harvest of bounty for You. Help me to avoid the bad seeds of hate, discouragement, and unconcern toward You. Help me to pay careful attention to what I am sowing in my life, so that everything I do will glorify and honor You.

Practical Parables
The first lesson of this parable is the simple principle of sowing and reaping. Just as a farmer will reap the results of his sowing, so a Christian will bear the consequences (good or ill) according to what he has done in his life.

What was the reason Jesus used this particular parable to teach His followers and disciples? We already know that Jesus used parables so that everyone in His audience could understand what He was saying. The youngest child there probably understood the principle of planting. They had watched their father plant in the fields around their home and then had seen him rejoice at harvest.

The word parable, *parabole* in the Greek, means "a similitude." A parable was a comparison with a fact or activity common to everyday life. A parable was fictitious but conveyed a truth. It was a way for Christ to teach God's exalted truths in a way that we could more fully understand.

For example, when Jesus gave the parable of the sower, the next time someone saw a farmer sowing or were planting themselves, they might think of what Jesus had said. So this truth had a way of penetrating not just immediately, but Jesus' words would come to mind later as the people listening did these activities themselves.

This was true of Carol. She hadn't been to church too often throughout her life; but one Christmas when she was eleven, she was invited to a Christmas pageant. The lights, the people playing Mary and Joseph, even a live donkey — all of this made a deep impression on her. Most Christmases, her grand-father dressed up as Santa Claus and distributed gifts to the children. No one mentioned the greatest Gift of all, Jesus Christ. She vowed in her earnest childishness that when she married and had children, she would seek to show them the true meaning of Christmas.

The first year she held her son, Josh, in her arms, she sought a church at Christmastime. It was a beautiful Christmas Eve service, and Carol sat in the back with baby Josh on her lap. Tears ran down her cheeks as she realized for the first time that Jesus Christ was born, and then lived and died for her. She trusted Him as her Savior during that service.

Carol never forgot that Christmas story she saw acted out. And that simple service was a help to her for the rest of her life. Jesus used parables for much the same reason: to make sure people understood what He was saying and to make such an impression on them that they never forgot the message.

Parables were given not to confuse but rather to confirm. They confirmed the important principles Christ conveyed. They confirmed His teaching in a personal, practical way that His followers and disciples could apply to their lives.

Resort Galilee

Look at the beginning of Mark chapter four. Take note of the setting the Lord chose for His teaching. He was sitting in a boat just a few feet from the shore of the Sea of Galilee.

And he began again to teach by the sea side: and there was gathered unto him a great multitude, so that he entered into a ship, and sat in the sea; and the whole multitude was by the sea on the land. Mark 4:1

I have visited the Sea of Galilee numerous times and love the beauty of that area. One unusual fact about that lake is that it is 700 feet below sea level. Surrounding the Sea of Galilee are mountains and because of the depth of the sea and its position, terrible storms can suddenly come upon it and cause huge waves like a sea — hence its name.

Ground Zero: Hearts of Stone

Why did Jesus use this parable? One of the reasons was because those opposing Him were becoming hostile. His adversaries, the Pharisees (the religious leaders of the day), were getting upset with Him and His teaching. Since the religious leaders were also, in many ways, the ruling leaders, the political climate was getting increasingly antagonistic toward Christ. To put this in modern-day lingo, if you polled the Pharisees on Jesus' popularity, Christ would have hardly registered!

Why were the Pharisees so angry at Jesus? They didn't like it that He could forgive sin. They realized that no one could forgive sin but God, so if Jesus could do that then He must be God. They didn't want to accept Him as God, so their hatred grew. They were upset because He spent time with publicans (tax collectors!) and sinners (Matthew 9:10–11). They refused to see His love and care for all mankind and said that Jesus did His miracles only by the power of the devil (John 10:20).

Count on the world to take the only perfect man and compare Him to the worst thing they know! We see this happening more and more in today's culture. Those who stand for righteousness are seen as the narrow religious right, while liberals are praised no matter what their actions. If this happened during the time of Christ, then why should we be surprised that it is happening today?

Growing hostility and opposition made it harder for Jesus to preach His doctrine plainly. Consequently, Jesus changed His method of teaching. Mark 3:5a reveals Jesus' attitude toward the Pharisees.

And when he had looked round about on them with anger, being grieved for the hardness of their hearts.... Mark 3:5a

The Lord Jesus wanted everyone to be saved, including the Pharisees, but they were hard-hearted. This grieved Jesus, and so He began to teach them, giving parables so they would have a picture of the truth.

When an art gallery opens, it takes people actually entering the studio before the artwork can be viewed. And so, as we examine the context of Jesus' day, the political and religious climate, we can view the picture of what Christ is saying. In subsequent chapters, we will be studying this parable or picture of truth, gleaning from it many practical truths and helps.

Our children need pictures and illustrations to help them learn and so do we. One of the ordinances the Lord gave to Christians to observe is called the Lord's Supper. This ceremony can be performed as often as a church likes, and there are no set rules about its observance. But it is important that you attend a church that practices the Lord's Supper, for this ceremony is a wonderful way for us to get a picture of what our Lord suffered on Calvary for us.

I remember the first time I took communion after I was saved. I silently prayed as I confessed my sin. I ate the cracker and in a physical way remembered the broken body of our Lord. Tears came to my eyes as I thought of His body, bruised and battered for me. Then when I drank the small cup of grape juice, I remembered His blood shed for me. It was almost more than I could bear; it was so emotionally moving. Every time I lead my own congregation in communion, I feel the same way. It takes me back to the day of my salvation and keeps me at the foot of the cross.

I challenge you to take part in a communion service as often as you can. For you need this picture of the Lord's death to remind you of the price He paid for your salvation. This will help you as you grow in your walk with the Lord.

"I'm not going to change!"
The Pharisees' hearts were like stone regardless of the method of teaching Jesus used. Imagine what would happen if you tried to plant a seed in a stone — it just wouldn't grow! While there were many Pharisees that believed on Christ (Nicodemus being one of them — John 3:1), there were many who didn't listen. Many chose instead to let their spiritual eyes stay blind, and their hearts became even more resistant to truth.

The story of two young sisters illustrates this hardness of heart. All day long, they'd been having verbal spats, each of them saying mean things. That night as they knelt down by the bed with their mother, the older girl prayed, "Lord, I want you to bless my mom and my dad and my dog and my cat. I want you to bless my parakeet and my goldfish…"

Mom cleared her throat, "Aren't you forgetting someone?"

"Oh yes," continued the girl, "I want you to bless my ex-sister."

We all know that even young children know what it means to hold a grudge! Get over that childish tendency in your own Christian life, and it will help you to change your heart of stone to soft soil ready for phenomenal growth.

Sometimes an incident that seems like no big deal can lead to the soil of our lives getting hard. Larry found this to be true in his own life. A divorced dad, he only went to the Baptist church in his area because he had full custody of his four-year-old daughter, Shelly. It had been a nasty divorce. Both parents made many terrible statements in the presence of their little girl. After the divorce, Larry determined that life would be better for his child and so he brought her to Sunday School.

When he went to pick her up, he found she loved Sunday School and wanted to attend the church service immediately following. Mainly because he didn't have anything else to do, he went. Sitting in that service, he heard things from the Bible he had never heard before. He realized that he hadn't even read a page of the Bible since his grandmother had told him Bible stories when he was younger than his own daughter. Shelly's dark head lay against his shoulder; and his heart, which he thought couldn't soften from the bitter break-up of his marriage, began to heal. When the pastor gave the gospel and explained that going to Heaven wasn't anything that anyone earns but instead was a gift from God, he trusted Christ.

This was the beginning of many church services for Larry and Shelly. One day the pastor approached Larry and asked him if he would mind doing some maintenance on the church grounds during the weekends. The janitor had a broken leg and couldn't work for awhile.

Larry didn't let it show, but he was angry that the pastor would ask such a thing of him. Didn't he realize that Larry barely had time to attend Sunday morning services at the church? He didn't have enough free time to spend with Shelly as it was. He didn't want more things to get in the way of their relationship.

Larry felt his heart harden with pride. He was about to refuse until he looked at Shelly's face. A huge smile told him that she wanted him to agree to the pastor's request.

"Daddy," Shelly exclaimed, "We can do it together! Remember how you showed me how to pull weeds from the flowerbeds? I could do that around the church yard while you mow the grass!"

Larry had to agree to the pastor's request. Later, he realized that his pride had almost messed up not only his own spiritual growth but the growth of his little girl. He vowed not to let that happen again.

Our hearts can become hardened so quickly because of pride. God wants us to have hearts that are moldable like clay, not hard like a rock.

Two men were best friends all through their growing-up years. They worked together at the same place for 50 years. One day, they had an argument and stopped speaking to each other. As things happen, their grandchildren became engaged. Both men knew that they had to get along if their grandchildren were going to be married, so they decided to forgive and forget. They couldn't even remember the reason they were angry with each other in the first place!

"I want to change, but how?"
Here is another tip on avoiding hard-heartedness. Don't rely solely on first impressions of a church service or meeting. Take time to

get to know the pastor and the people. Many people let their first impression of a church dictate their future participation. Don't be like the man who bit into his first banana just as his train went through a tunnel. The man determined never to eat bananas again because they caused temporary blindness!

Go to several services before you conclude anything. Attend more than just Sunday morning; attend anytime there is a service. Bible-believing and teaching churches don't have just one "mass" that is the same for each service. Each service is its own separate experience where you will hear a different sermon from the pastor. Attending all the services will help you make a more complete determination about whether the church will help you in your spiritual growth.

Volunteer your help in the different ministries of the church. After a month or two, decide if the church is one in which you may grow in your Christian life. If it is, stick with it!

The Christian life can be viewed similar to the way a sporting event is observed. The way a fan watches a basketball game is in contrast to the way a player observes the same contest. The player is waiting for the opportunity to get into the game while the fan watches only with great interest. In a local church, we need to be more like players and less like spectators. We need to participate in the action rather than sitting back and offering commentary on the way others play.

Jesus said in Matthew 13:16, *But blessed are your eyes, for they see: and your ears, for they hear.* In the realm of the spiritual, what are you doing with your eyes and ears? Are you using your eyes to read Scripture and observe other mature Christians' lives in the hopes of modeling yourself after them? Are you using your ears to hear the Word of God as it is preached and apply those principles to your life?

When our senses are keenly in tune with the things of God, then we will avoid the hardness of heart Jesus was talking about. Our heart will be softened and ready to receive the great truths God would have us learn. Open your heart right now to His Word.

Essential Nutrients for Growth

And he taught them many things by parables, and said unto them in his doctrine, Mark 4:2.

I have heard some Christians remark that Jesus is not interested in doctrine. They claim that doctrine is not worth fighting over. Instead, we should fellowship with anyone and everyone if they simply name the name of Jesus. This is a dangerous philosophy, for it is doctrine upon which all of Scripture rests.

The word "doctrine" means "instruction." It refers to the teaching that is in Scripture. If we are not concerned about doctrine, then we are rejecting teaching. If there is anything worth fighting for, it is the teachings of Christ. Everything He uttered was for our good and instruction (Romans 15:4).

So take a moment right now and pray that you will understand these teachings of our Lord. Understand that He understands and knows your heart. Pray that as you study this parable, it will help you in every aspect of your growth as a Christian.

God's Curriculum

When we first trust Christ, there are many hard and difficult things about the Word of God that we cannot understand; but we have God's promise to enlighten our minds, if we diligently search it out. Every day that we walk with God, He will show us more and more things about Himself.

When I trusted Christ during my senior year in college, the first thing I realized is now I wanted to read the Bible. Whereas before I considered the Bible a dull book without meaning, now I saw it as a living book full of truths I needed to learn.

Even now, there are passages of Scripture that I've read hundreds of times, yet I continue to learn new things from them. I have been a pastor for over 40 years. I have preached at least three or four sermons a week for much of that time. And yet, the more I learn, the more I want to learn. That is how God's Word is.

Perhaps this has happened in your own life. Maybe you grew up in some type of religion, yet you didn't have the desire to read the Bible. Now that you know Christ as your Savior, the Holy Spirit promises to guide you into all truth (John 16:13). Isaiah 45:3 explains that when we study the Word, it is like finding treasures in a secret place.

And I will give thee the treasures of darkness, and hidden riches of secret places, that thou mayest know that I, the LORD, which call thee by thy name, am the God of Israel.

Perhaps your children have participated in a "treasure hunt" at a birthday party or other event. An adult writes down clues that lead to a treasure. Each clue brings the children one step closer to their prize. It is the same way with the Word of God. Each time we read a portion of it, we are brought a step closer in our relationship with the Lord. Therefore, we need to continue to make the study of His Word a priority in our daily schedule.

Take a moment to pray this prayer.

Thank you, Lord, for giving me Your Word. Help me to read it and pay attention to what it says. I pray that I will give the study of the Bible sufficient time in my busy schedule. Help me to make Your Word a priority so I can continue to prepare the soil of my life for spiritual growth.

WHAT MAKES A CHRISTIAN GROW?

The Christian life is a laboratory course, not a lecture course.
~Anonymous~

Prepare for Progress

When I was 13 years old, I enjoyed working at my brother-in-law's farm in Oklahoma. I remember those hot summers as some of the best moments of my life. I felt privileged to drive a tractor and make a dollar an hour (top money in those days!). I drove the tractor the first twelve hours of the day and my brother-in-law drove it the other twelve hours. We never shut it off. We fueled the tractor in the field so we would never have to stop working. I felt lonely out there at times, but knowing that my uncle trusted me to do such an important job kept me going.

In the same way, we see Jesus entrusting His disciples with the great truth found in Mark chapter four. The people listening to Him probably didn't realize it fully at the time, but the parable of the sower would give them practical help as they grew in their Christian lives.

Mark 4:3 states, *Hearken; Behold, there went out a sower to sow:*

Observe that the farmer is planting the seeds for a reason. He is expecting the seeds to take root in the ground and for them to bear fruit.

Land was at a premium in the days of Jesus (and even today!). Anyone who has traveled to Israel knows that there is more rocky soil than fertile soil. On a trip to Israel, a farmer who owns thousands of acres in the United States told me how astounded he was that there was so little good soil in Israel. And he was surprised at how inventive the people are at fully utilizing the land they do have.

Do you feel sometimes that you are one of only a few Christians in your workplace? Do you feel sometimes like others in your family consider your beliefs a bit strange? Just as there wasn't much good soil in which the farmer could sow seed in the parable we are studying, so it is true that the culture around us is anti-Christian in many ways.

Matthew 7:13–14 states, *Enter ye in at the strait gate: for wide is the gate, and broad is the way, that leadeth to destruction, and many there be which go in thereat: Because strait is the gate, and narrow is the way, which leadeth unto life, and few there be that find it.*

Why are there few who enter in at the strait gate? Because the god of this world, Satan, has fooled people into believing that it is their good works that bring them eternal life. 2 Corinthians 4:4 states, *In whom the god of this world hath blinded the minds of them which believe not, lest the light of the glorious gospel of Christ, who is the image of God, should shine unto them.*

So don't be surprised when your colleague makes fun of your beliefs. Understand that they are only reacting that way because they are still depending on their works for salvation. Pray daily for that person and go out of your way to be kind to them. Maybe someday they will trust Christ as their Savior.

The day Andrea trusted Christ was the happiest day of her life. A college friend took the time to explain the plan of salvation to her. The following morning, Andrea drove four hours to spend some time with her family over the weekend. Thrilled with her decision, Andrea lost no time in telling her family members that now she knew she was "saved."

"Saved?" Andrea's brother, Bob, snorted. "I didn't know you were lost."

"I mean that I don't have to worry about going to Hell anymore. I have been saved from my sin." Andrea said.

"Andrea, please!" Bob begged, "I'm sick of this stuff. I'm sure you'll get over this religious kick in time."

To say Andrea felt hurt would be an understatement. She didn't understand why her family didn't want to hear about her wonderful Lord. She was tempted to get discouraged, but her friend from college explained that it would take time for her family to see the difference in Andrea. She involved herself in a church near her college campus. Slowly the family's attitude changed. A year or so later, Andrea experienced the joy of leading her brother to Christ.

A Seed Called Study
Do you place yourself in situations where the seed of the Word of God can be sown in your life? Do you go to church services whenever possible, so that you can hear the Bible preached? Do you read the Bible daily, so that you can glean eternal truth?

Vicky grew up in a Christian home and trusted Christ at a young age. Yet, there always seemed to be something lacking in her Christian life. She couldn't quite put her finger on what was wrong until she heard a sermon about having daily devotions. She realized that she hadn't allowed enough of the Word of God to permeate her soul.

Now she spends 15 minutes to a half hour each morning reading a passage of Scripture before she goes to work. She started with the Gospels and then read through the book of Philippians. Now when problems occur during her day, she remembers the verses she read that morning. It is easier for her to handle hardships, and she feels she has found the missing component to growing in her spiritual journey.

Perhaps you are like Vicky and haven't considered reading the Bible on a daily basis. It might seem like this is difficult to schedule in at first. Know that Satan will be waiting with a thousand distractions to keep you from doing it! But when you systematically take time to study Scripture, you will grow in your Christian life. You will be allowing the seed of the Word of God to penetrate deep into your heart.

A Seed Called Preaching

With a light spiritual diet and diminishing personal discipline, many Christians have decided that attending church is not important. *U.S. News and World Report* says that eight of every ten Americans today believe that it's possible to be a good Christian or Jew without attending a church or synagogue. Increasing numbers of people are either staying away from church or identifying with church at arm's length. With larger congregations today, it's easy to say you attend such-and-such church while remaining anonymous. Perhaps no one there even knows you personally.[1]

Yet the importance of regularly attending a Bible-believing church can hardly be emphasized enough! There is a tremendous difference in spiritual growth between those Christians who attend church and those who don't! How could there not be? When a person exposes themselves to as much of the Word of God through their own personal study and from as many other sources as they possibly can, the chance for growth increases exponentially.

Some of the people who attend our church regularly now tell me that before they came out to church, their Christian life was in a slump. There would be times they would feel convicted to do something about their backward spiritual direction, yet they lacked accountability and the teaching to change. Now that they attend church, they are able to systematically grow. When I preach on issues that they are facing in the office, they feel encouraged to keep plugging along. When I explain difficult Bible verses to them, they can use that explanation to help others.

One couple attended our Sunday morning service for over ten years before they came to any other services. It took time for them to understand the importance of getting as much of the Word of God as they could. Now that they regularly come to every service, they often tell me how much the sermons have helped them in their walk with Christ.

If you haven't yet found a Bible-believing-and-teaching church, then I encourage you to do so today. If you aren't as involved as you should be in a good church, then decide right now to be more faithful. You will find the weekly strengthening absolutely necessary for your spiritual quest.

The Lonely Sower
We've looked at the soil; now let's look at the sower. Farming, especially in those days, was a lonely occupation. But the farmer knew one thing: The hard work that he put into the soil would eventually pay off through the survival of his family. This kept him going in spite of the heat, the rain, and the daily hardships of his life.

Do you sometimes feel like this lonely sower? No matter how many verses you memorize or how much you pray, it doesn't seem like there is fruit for your labor? Think about the farmer in the parable Jesus told. He faithfully sowed the seed and let God worry about the harvest. This is the way it is in the Christian life. It is our job to remain faithful, and it is His job to bring the harvest.

We are like children sometimes, impatient to see results before sufficient time has passed. I think of our preschool and the many years we had gardens for the children to tend. Whenever the children would go out to weed and water their plots, it was difficult for them not to pluck up the plants by the roots to "see" how they were doing! They wanted instant results and had a hard time learning to wait for what seemed to them slow growth.

Know that just as the child needs to wait for the plant to grow, so we need to wait for God's harvest. Don't be discouraged as you wait. Instead continue to sow the seed of the Word of God. He has guaranteed us the harvest, but this harvest is up to Him, not us.

1 Corinthians 3:6–7 explains this. *I have planted, Apollos watered; but God gave the increase. So then neither is he that planteth any thing, neither he that watereth; but God that giveth the increase.*

The sower could also be compared to the preacher of a local church. He can feel lonely at times as he patiently sows the Word of God. But the man who sows by himself often blesses many. Thousands reap what was sown alone. Some of that seed will fall onto stone and the birds will come and take it. Some will fall on trampled paths, which are so hardened that nothing will change it. Some of that seed will fall on good ground, which produces a harvest of mature Christians.

Proper Preparation
What is the single-best indicator that seed will germinate properly? The field first needs proper preparation. The field needs to be good, soft dirt that will readily receive the seed and allow the seed to grow strong.

This is true in our own lives as well. We need to first prepare our own hearts before we can receive the Word of God in a proper way. We need to take the time to pray, "Lord, I want to receive Your Word and what it has to say. I want to understand it and then apply it to my life."

Then when we read a portion of the Bible, the Holy Spirit will help us to understand it and thereby apply it. The seed will produce a lot more if it is sown in the proper type of soil.

Sarah and Michael had attended First Baptist Church for about a year. Coming from another denominational background, they were unprepared at first for the differences of First Baptist. The preaching was the biggest dissimilarity. Their first church was liberal, and the preacher never preached strongly. This never bothered them before they got saved, but now they realized they needed to learn more about the Word of God. When a friend invited them to try her church, they didn't hesitate.

The preacher encouraged everyone to bring their Bibles to church; but when Michael asked Sarah where their Bible was, Sarah was embarrassed to admit that she didn't know. She hadn't looked at their Bible since the day they were married and had recorded that important date on the front page. After much searching, Sarah finally found the Bible under a stack of old *National Geographic* magazines. Hesitantly at first, because he had never attempted such a thing, Michael opened the Bible to the book of Matthew and read a chapter or so every night.

The first week they brought their Bible to church, they listened as the preacher asked his congregation to turn to the book of Ecclesiastes. Sarah opened the Bible and thumbed through the strange names attempting to find Ecclesiastes. Finally, she gave up and handed the book to Michael. He flipped through the book ten times in his attempt to find it. Finally, suppressing a grin at their predicament, Sarah opened the book to the index. Running her finger down the book titles, she finally found the gold mine, Ecclesiastes! She shot a triumphant glance at her husband as she noted the page number and turned the pages until she reached the correct one. Then the preacher announced that he wanted everyone to turn to Leviticus, and Michael and Sarah almost groaned out loud! Leviticus! They had just finally found Ecclesiastes!

If you could see Michael and Sarah in their pew at First Baptist Church now, you would never know that at one time they hardly knew where their Bible was, much less where any of the books were located. They flip through the pages like pros, helping each other as they follow along with the pastor's message.

Michael and Sarah have learned one of the secrets for growth. They didn't allow their own embarrassment to keep them from trying to learn the Word of God. They took time to prepare the soil of their hearts, to first study the Bible together each night and then to learn where each of the books was located. Even though it was difficult at first, their effort resulted in a better opportunity for growth, and this is the principle that we can learn through this parable.

Together with God
The Christian life is a partnership. God does the miraculous part, but we must prepare ourselves. Sometimes the process of growth is going to be painful. The seed, the Word of God, will reach into our lives and point out areas that need changing. Sometimes we are going to have to do something that is good for us spiritually, even though we may not like it.

When he was five years old, my grandson, Jamie, liked a lot of foods that other kids didn't, but sometimes even he would come across something he didn't like. One day it was mussels. They were part of a delicious buffet at a Japanese restaurant; but when I put some on his plate, he got a look that told me he didn't like the shellfish. I asked him if he had ever tried this dish and he said no. So I encouraged him to taste it. I told him, "Jamie, if you eat mussels, then maybe you will get muscles!" (I know that's corny, but it worked!) Even at 5, Jamie was an athletic boy, and one of his desires was to have strong muscles. So he popped the meat into his mouth. I was surprised when he said he liked it. Now mussels are one of his favorite foods!

When we feed on the Word of God, we produce spiritual muscle. This muscle will help us to continue serving the Lord even when hardships and trials come. 1 Peter 2:2–3 says, *As newborn babes, desire the sincere milk of the word, that ye may grow thereby: If so be ye have tasted that the Lord is gracious.*

When I was a boy working in the Oklahoma fields, I couldn't wait to hear what kind of wheat crop was harvested. Our goal was to always get thirty bushels per acre, and I couldn't wait to see what the yield was going to be.

I love these verses about sowing and reaping.

They that sow in tears shall reap in joy. He that goeth forth and weepeth, bearing precious seed, shall doubtless come again with rejoicing, bringing his sheaves with him. Psalm 126:5–6

But this I say, He which soweth sparingly shall reap also sparingly; and he which soweth bountifully shall reap also bountifully. 2 Corinthians 9:6

There once was a beggar who would sit every day in the street and beg for rice. As people passed, they would drop a kernel or two of rice into his bowl. Each day he received just enough to survive.

One day the beggar was sitting with his little collection of rice when a Maharajah walked past. The beggar was sure that the Maharajah would be generous. He was sure the Maharajah would fill his bowl full of rice.

The Maharajah came to the beggar and said, "I want what you have in your bowl."

The beggar thought, *I have nothing and this rich man wants me to give him the only rice I have.*

The beggar took one kernel of rice from the bowl and threw it at the wealthy man in disgust. The Maharajah said, "I want more."

The beggar took one more kernel of rice and threw it to the Maharajah. Again, the Maharajah said, "I want more."

Again the beggar threw him another kernel. The Maharajah then took out of his pocket three grams of gold. He gave the beggar a gram of gold for every kernel of rice given to him.

As the Maharajah returned to his carriage he thought, *Could not this man have spared more?*

The beggar stared at his three grams of gold realizing that if he had just been generous, he could be holding a whole bowlful of gold.

Many times we act like that beggar. We cling to our old ways instead of trying God's ways. We grasp our own ideas instead of studying the Scripture to understand His ideas. As a result, we fail to experience the blessing of growth in our lives.

Take a moment right now and think about yourself. Are you willing to do things God's way so that you will grow in your faith? Are you willing to prepare the soil of your heart so that God can bring His precious seed to maturity?

Are you attending a church only a few times a month? If you are, then decide right now to prepare the soil by going as often as you can. Are you spending time in Bible reading and prayer? If you aren't, then block out fifteen minutes of your day for this all-important part of growth. Freeing up your schedule will prepare the soil of your life to receive the life-giving seed of the Word.

Crunch Time

Once when Michigan State was playing UCLA in football, the score was tied at 14 with only seconds to play. Duffy Daugherty, Michigan State's coach, sent in place-kicker, Dave Kaiser, who booted a field goal that won the game. When the kicker returned to the bench, Daugherty said, "Nice going, but you didn't watch the ball after you kicked it."

"That's right, Coach," Kaiser replied. "I was watching the referee instead to see how he'd signal it. I forgot my contact lenses, and I couldn't see the goal posts."[2]

Kaiser was fortunate that he had made that crucial point. Forgetting his contact lenses could have cost his team the game. The importance of preparation in every area of our lives can hardly be emphasized enough. It is the same way in the Christian life. It is crucial that we prepare the soil for optimal spiritual growth.

Hosea 10:12 states, *Sow to yourselves in righteousness, reap in mercy; break up your fallow ground: for it is time to seek the LORD, till he come and rain righteousness upon you.*

Famous missionary, Hudson Taylor, said, "I used to ask God to come and help me. I realized how wrong that was and now I ask, God, may I come and help You? May You do Your work through me."

The Word of God is powerful when nurtured. If it sits, then our lives will stagnate. We will not get anything out of it.

The growth of a Christian is determined by the way they prepare their souls. Take some time right now and assess your spiritual growth. Are you preparing the soil of your own heart? Are you working to weed out appointments and activities that could keep you from having ample time to receive the Word of God? Ask the Lord to help you prepare the soil of your heart for exciting, productive, and lifelong growth!

-3-

The Peril of Shallow Soil

Be a stand-by for the Lord, not merely a bystander.
~Anonymous~

Mark had prayed for a long time for an opportunity to speak to one of his fellow engineers about Christ. However, it seemed like the chance never came. One day Mark decided to take Fred out for lunch. They didn't have much time, for they were both working on an all-consuming project. Right away Mark opened the conversation. He then began to give him the gospel.

Fred listened for about a half minute but interjected his own comments. He asked some questions that had no bearing on the topic, effectively side-tracking Mark. When it was time to go back to work, Fred thanked Mark for the lunch and said, "Listen Mark, this religious stuff is okay for you; but it isn't my cup of tea, if you know what I mean. I would appreciate it if you didn't talk about it anymore."

Mark felt disappointed, but he honored Fred's wishes. Later Mark shared with me how his conversation went with Fred. Because I was studying the parable of the sower, I opened my Bible and explained that Jesus had predicted this exact situation. When the seed is sown, some of it falls on the wayside; and before it can germinate, Satan comes and snatches the seed, preventing that person's salvation.

Mark 4:4 explains, *And it came to pass, as he sowed, some fell by the way side, and the fowls of the air came and devoured it up.*

Mark 4:15 details, *And these are they by the way side, where the word is sown; but when they have heard, Satan cometh immediately, and taketh away the word that was sown in their hearts.*

I encouraged Mark to continue to pray for more witnessing opportunities and not to be discouraged from his last attempt. Just as the sower's job is to sow the seed, so that is every Christian's job. Some seed will fall by the wayside; there is no way to avoid this. But if we diligently continue, then we can be assured that some seed will find nurturing soil.

Perfect Too Soon

Janet enjoyed her busy life. Shuttling her kids to soccer games and school, she managed to develop friendships with many of the other mothers who were in the same position. As she cheered for her daughters, she prayed she would use given opportunities to share her faith. One day, in a casual conversation with another mother named Serena, Janet finally had her chance. She described first her own inward emptiness before she knew Christ. She explained that she wondered if she even had a purpose in life. When she learned of Christ's death on the cross and how it paid the penalty for her sin, she realized that all she needed to do was to accept His gift of salvation in order to have eternal life.

Janet was surprised when Serena listened attentively. Janet expected her to at least ask questions about what she was saying. As the soccer game ended, Janet asked her friend if she wanted to receive Christ. Serena immediately said yes. Janet made sure that Serena understood the gospel and realized that there was nothing she could do for her own salvation.

That night as Janet drove her daughters home, a deep joy abode in her heart. She was glad the Lord had given her the opportunity to witness to Serena and that her friend had trusted Christ.

Serena couldn't seem to talk to Janet enough after that. Every soccer practice and game, the two could be seen earnestly conversing, a Bible open between them. Serena began attending Janet's church and the two spent even more time together. Janet learned that Serena had been married twice before and now was trying to raise two daughters, both from her first marriage.

The two grew close. Janet prayed daily for Serena that she would continue to grow in her faith. Then one day Serena didn't show up for church. Concerned, Janet called her friend. Not finding her at home, she called the next day. But it seemed like Serena and her daughters had dropped off the ends of the earth.

A month later, Janet called and was surprised when Serena answered. At first Serena seemed hesitant to talk, but finally she told Janet what had been going on. A man from her past had shown up and on impulse, Serena began to date him. A whirlwind courtship ensued, and now she was married. Serena didn't seem interested in talking very long, and Janet was at a loss for words. She asked Serena if she was planning to come back to church, and Serena said she had thought about it but probably would not return. She said that church attendance had been taking up too much of her time; and while she wasn't against coming occasionally, she said that she needed to get on with her life.

As Janet hung up the phone, she felt devastated. How could Serena have made such a bad decision, marrying an unbeliever? She didn't know if she would ever figure it out.

Janet would be comforted to know that Jesus talked about just such a person when He gave the parable of the sower and the seed. He described Serena and thousands like her (both men and women) who become "perfect too soon."

Mark 4:5 states, *And some fell on stony ground, where it had not much earth; and immediately it sprang up, because it had no depth of earth.*

Mark 4:16–17 gives us the explanation of this situation, *And these are they likewise which are sown on stony ground; who, when they have heard the word, immediately receive it with gladness; And have no root in themselves, and so endure but for a time: afterward, when affliction or persecution ariseth for the word's sake, immediately they are offended.*

These verses speak about people who receive the Word with gladness. They experience a great spurt of growth in the beginning of their Christian experience, but then wither away. There is danger to the Christian who grows very quickly in Christ. I don't mean that growth is not something that is expected. 1 Timothy 3:6 describes this well. *Not a novice, lest being lifted up with pride he fall into the condemnation of the devil.* If the plant is not rooted and grounded in sound doctrine, when the inevitable hardships come, the excitement will die off and the once-vibrant Christian will wither away.

Does this mean that this peaked-out believer loses their salvation? The Bible is clear that once a person has trusted Christ, they are saved forever. Nothing can loosen the grip of God's hand. John 10:28 says, *And I give unto them eternal life; and they shall never perish, neither shall any man pluck them out of my hand.* But growth in Christ will stop, and they will fail to experience the blessings that God wants to bestow upon their life.

Watch Out: Construction Ahead!
I remember when my friend, Stan's, son, Jerry, got his driver's license. Jerry proudly showed it to me the day he got it. Stan told me about when Jerry first got his permit. Excited to get behind the wheel, Jerry drove while Stan sat in the passenger seat. Stan's nerves were on edge; but after awhile, he realized that Jerry really was a pretty good driver.

Then the sky got darker, and Stan saw that it was going to storm. He warned Jerry that the first few minutes of a rain are the most dangerous because the oil on the road makes the road slippery.

Jerry seemed to take this pretty well. Concentrating on the approaching storm, Stan did not heed the signs that proclaimed they were in a construction area. Forgetting that he had heard on the radio just that morning about a zero-tolerance policy going into effect for failure to heed construction warnings, Stan didn't say anything to Jerry. Flashing lights behind them brought panic to both Jerry and Stan. Jerry pulled the car to the side of the road and looked inquiringly at his dad. What was it that he had done wrong? He was traveling the speed limit. The police officer explained that Jerry should have slowed down as soon sas he saw the warning sign. To Stan's chagrin, Jerry had to get a ticket because of the new policy that had just been passed.

It took Jerry an extra year to get his driver's license after that. So you can understand why Jerry was so proud when he finally got his license!

Just as Stan missed the warning because of an approaching storm, it is easy to miss God's warnings. We cruise down life's freeway oblivious to the orange signs until we see the flashing lights. Then we quickly pull over and take a quick, personal assessment, realizing that we had been given warning after warning but had tragically failed to heed them.

The word "offended" in Mark 4:17 is the Greek word *skandalizo*, and it means "to entrap or trip up." Persecution or difficulty is like a tiny cable that stretches across our path. If we fail to heed the orange signs, the wire is sure to make us lose our footing.

All of us will be offended from time to time. It is an undeniable fact of our daily life. A boss is going to say something that rubs us the wrong way. A spouse will utter a sarcastic comment after we've had a particularly bad day. Our children will say something that embarrasses us in front of our friends. But we don't have to let these offenses take hold of our lives and carry us away from God's purpose and plan.

The ability to get offended can measure the depth of our spirituality. I've known some Christians who just couldn't seem to get off the ground spiritually because they were easily offended. But if we allow God's Word to penetrate our souls, then petty circumstances cannot deter us from truehearted service.

The people described in this passage get all excited in the beginning of their walk of faith. When they first trust Christ, they are like Serena, eager to serve the Lord. But as soon as something happens at work to deter their faith or a fellow church member makes a sarcastic statement, they back away from the Lord.

Jesus explains that their lack of solid roots keeps them from staying grounded in spite of the offense. While they are still saved, they have not let the Word get through to their hearts, their innermost soul. Luke 8:6 says, *And some fell upon a rock; and as soon as it was sprung up, it withered away, because it lacked moisture.* So the problem is two-fold. First, the roots have not gone far below the surface; and second, because of that, the moisture wasn't able to nourish the root.

From my summers in Oklahoma, I understand how important moisture is to a crop. We would take a special piece of farming equipment called a "one-way," and go over that whole field. Our purpose was to break up the dirt so that the water stayed in the ground. As a result, the wheat would have more moisture, producing a better yield.

How do we let the one-way of God's Word keep us from the terrible scenario of the lack of roots and moisture? First, we need to pray that God would give us soft hearts towards His Word. We need to stay in a humble frame of mind so that the life-giving power of God's Word can transform us from the inside out.

Dear friend, are you in danger of letting the daily cares and difficulties of your life keep you from Christian growth? Take a moment right now and ask God to humble your own heart. Ask for His healing to counteract the world's affliction and His strength to handle Satan's darts. You can be sure that when you do this, the seed of the Word will be allowed to sink roots in your own heart so you rise to perform great service for Him.

Rude Awakening

A practical way to ensure deep roots in our faith is to observe the two ordinances our Lord gave to every believer. The first is the Lord's Supper, or Communion. I wrote about this earlier. A Bible-believing-and-teaching church will have this ceremony at least several times a year. We do it once a month. The Bible isn't specific about how often we should do it, rather it states that we should do it as often as we like, until He comes again. 1 Corinthians 11:26 explains, *For as often as ye eat this bread, and drink this cup, ye do shew the Lord's death till he come.*

The second ordinance that every Christian needs to observe is water baptism. We perform this first because our Lord was baptized when He was upon this earth. Matthew 3:16 explains, *And Jesus, when he was baptized, went up straightway out of the water: and, lo, the heavens were opened unto him, and he saw the Spirit of God descending like a dove, and lighting upon him:*

Water baptism is a way that we can identify with our Lord in His death, burial, and resurrection. Romans 6:4 states, *Therefore we are buried with him by baptism into death: that like as Christ was raised up from the dead by the glory of the Father, even so we also should walk in newness of life.* Water baptism is an outward showing of what has happened on the inside.

Anna was a Christian before she married Carl. She thought she was so in love with him that it didn't matter that he didn't know Christ. But after their three children came along, she found that it did matter, a lot. She wanted to take the children to church, yet Carl resisted her at every turn. Night after night, she cried after she tucked her daughter and two sons into bed. She hadn't been to church for so long, she almost couldn't remember how to pray. So her prayers with her children were halting and stilted. She wanted so much to experience the fellowship and blessing she had felt when she had attended church as a teenager, but Carl was dead set against it.

One day, a shaken Carl came home early from work. Anna asked what was wrong. One of the safety belts that kept Carl's window-washing associate safe had come loose. Plunging twenty stories, the man tore through a large awning on the third floor. Fortunately, this broke the man's fall enough that he ended up with only a few broken bones. As Carl hurried down his own scaffolding, he assumed the worst. He told Anna that at that moment, he realized there was something missing in his life.

The family started attending a Bible-believing church; and after a few weeks of hearing the gospel, Carl accepted Christ. A month or so later, at the end of the morning service, the pastor gave an invitation for water baptism.

Carl had never heard of this ordinance before and when he went home, he asked Anna about it. Anna explained that she had been baptized when she was a teenager and that water baptism was telling the world what Jesus Christ had done for him. Carl decided that he wanted to be water baptized, but it took him four more Sundays to get up the courage to walk forward. That evening, the pastor shared another verse with him. 1 Peter 3:21 states, *The like figure whereunto even baptism doth also now save us (not the putting away of the filth of the flesh, but the answer of a good conscience toward God,) by the resurrection of Jesus Christ:*

Later, the preacher said, "Carl, based on your profession of faith in Christ, I baptize you in the name of the Father, the Son, and the Holy Spirit." Carl felt tears come to his eyes. He was beginning to understand that knowing Jesus Christ had made all the difference. As he came up out of the water, he felt exhilarated, glad that he had made this decision to follow the Lord.

In our church, you can either come forward on a Sunday morning to say you want to be water baptized, or you can come privately to one of our leadership staff. In other churches you could speak to the preacher about your desire. Making the decision to be water baptized is important in the life of growth. Following this ordinance from our Lord will help your roots anchor tightly so that when difficulties come, you will better withstand their unavoidable assault.

Disabling Difficulties

And have no root in themselves, and so endure but for a time: afterward, when affliction or persecution ariseth for the word's sake, immediately they are offended. Mark 4:17

Not long ago, I traveled with a great friend, Jack Turney, to India. My son-in-law, Neal, and two other men from our Bible college also went with us. The wonderful people of India welcomed us, and we ministered to them. Jack brought a well-drilling rig with him in the hopes of drilling a well near the compound where we stayed. The rig was completely unassembled, and it took Neal and the other two guys quite a few days of hard work to get the rig together. When the drilling began, it seemed at first like it was going great. But fifteen feet or so down, they hit solid rock, and the drilling slowed to inches per hour. Eventually, it was decided that this type of well driller would work only in a place that didn't have so much rock.

Many people are like the ground beneath that compound in India. At first, the Word of God gets through to them and they get excited. But a few weeks or even years later, they harden their heart to the Word. Perhaps they get tired of the ridicule from other people at work. Maybe they don't like their own family's lack of understanding toward their faith. And instead of digging deeper and breaking up the rocky soil of their heart, they stop growing in their walk with Christ.

Have you let afflictions and persecutions keep you from fully serving Christ? Have you stopped attending church as regularly as you used to because of your own discouragement? Is your prayer life not what it ought to be because you have let unbelievers discourage you? Have you halted your daily quiet time with the Lord? Take some time right now to break up those rocks of resistance in your own heart and let the water of God's Word flood your life with peace.

Danger! The Big Three Could Choke You!

You must leave your possessions behind when God summons.
~Yiddish Proverb~

In only ten months, 28 pedestrians were killed crossing the streets of San Francisco, making it the state's most dangerous walking city. The city's rate of pedestrian deaths and injuries, 124 per 100,000 residents, is nearly triple that of second-place Los Angeles.

"We're the center of a rushed, dot-com industry," says City Supervisor, Mabel Teng, sponsor of various pedestrian initiatives. "This is a city in transition, but it needs to remain livable."[1]

The high rate of pedestrian deaths is yet another example of our rushed culture. Many counties have passed laws banning the use of cell phones while driving because of people failing to pay attention to what is around them. Countless "labor-saving" devices have been invented since the Industrial Revolution; and yet in some ways, these have created more work than ever. The rush to get big on Wall Street, keep up with the Joneses, and live what we call the "good life" crowds out important core values and keeps us from serving the Lord in the way that we should.

Jesus warned His followers of this in Mark 4:7, *And some fell among thorns, and the thorns grew up, and choked it, and it yielded no fruit.*

Mark 4:18–19 gives further explanation, *And these are they which are sown among thorns; such as hear the word. And the cares of this world, and the deceitfulness of riches, and the lusts of other things entering in, choke the word, and it becometh unfruitful.*

The Lord gives us some topics to watch out for in our spiritual journeys. These obstacles hinder our effectiveness, choke us spiritually, and keep us from focusing on Christ. Let's study the "Big Three."

- Creeping Cares
- The Sham of Worldly Success
- Counterfeit Cravings

Creeping Cares
As he wrote to the Roman believers, Paul understood how the cares of this world could choke our service to the Lord. He spoke of this in Romans 7:19–25.

For the good that I would I do not: but the evil which I would not, that I do. Now if I do that I would not, it is no more I that do it, but sin that dwelleth in me. I find then a law, that, when I would do good, evil is present with me. For I delight in the law of God after the inward man: But I see another law in my members, warring against the law of my mind, and bringing me into captivity to the law of sin which is in my members. O wretched man that I am! who shall deliver me from the body of this death? I thank God through Jesus Christ our Lord. So then with the mind I myself serve the law of God; but with the flesh the law of sin.

For years when the guys brought porn into the office, Al didn't mind. But the day he trusted Christ as his Savior, he began to be bothered by it. He tried to avoid the material as much as he could, but found it difficult because it was so readily available. He came to one of our pastors for counseling; and through much prayer and Bible study, Al began to understand that the Christian life is a battleground.

When Al trusted Christ as his Savior, he was given a new nature. This spiritual nature is actually God, the Holy Spirit, living within him. As Al learned to yield himself to his new nature, he saw himself becoming more like Christ.

The problem is that even though Al now had the Holy Spirit living within him, he still had the carnal nature with which he was born. This part of Al is called the "flesh." This doesn't refer to the skin covering our bodies, rather it refers to the part of our being that wants to sin and do what Satan would have us do instead of obeying Christ.

When Al began to realize that there was now a battle going on inside of him, he began to see that by gratifying his flesh, he was weakening his effectiveness to serve. He was letting the temptations of this world keep him from living victoriously. As he studied Scripture and attended church, he learned to allow himself to be led by the Spirit. This helped him to grow stronger in his faith.

One day, Al politely asked if the guys would stop bringing porn around him. He didn't think they would listen. To his surprise, the men respected his decision. One of his colleagues came up to Al later and shamefacedly explained that he was a Christian, but that nobody else would know it by the way he had been living. When Al had come forward so boldly, he had felt ashamed. He asked Al if they could hold each other accountable to keep their flesh from gaining control. Al agreed, and now on break, the two men spend time studying Scripture. They know that at anytime they could fall back into their old lifestyles, so they continue to guard against that happening.

Al and his friend have learned one of the secrets of the Christian life: the creeping temptations of the world around us can seriously hinder our progress. Like Al, learn to keep the first of the Big Three from choking you to death.

The Sham of Worldly Success

He was so excited. He knew he was going to Heaven. He had never been happier. Getting to know the Apostle Paul was wonderful. He was the first person to really care about him. Demas enjoyed working with Paul, helping him in many ways. But he kept thinking about what he wanted for his life. He desired a certain level of prestige, and it didn't seem like being a Christian brought him the success he craved. We read in 2 Timothy 4:10a, *For Demas hath forsaken me, having loved this present world, and is departed unto Thessalonica….*

Desires for worldly success present a barrier to letting the Word of God grow in us. This even happened to someone who worked beside the Apostle Paul! If these desires tempted someone working with Paul, they will certainly tempt us.

Unlike those represented by the ground beside the road, these do hear initially, and agree. Unlike those represented by the rocky ground, their understanding of the truth deepens. But eventually, they reject the truth; they do not continue to act on the truth because their stronger desires are for success in this world.

All of us act this way at times. We may understand a lot of Scripture and obey it. Our understanding of truth may have grown throughout the years, and we may feel that we are going along pretty well. Then the pastor says something that rubs us the wrong way. Maybe he presents a Biblical truth that we can't ignore. But we say, "Let's be practical. Surely God doesn't mean for me to do that! I might lose my job!"

Or we might say, "Yes, I can obey God in that area — after I make enough money and attain financial security."

Here's another statement we might make, "Wow, that's such a noble sentiment — but it's simply not practical. Maybe people 2,000 years ago could act that way, but it doesn't work in the 21st century."

All of us have responded to truth in this way at times, and it is important we guard against this temptation. Don't swallow the worldly sentiment that wealth is more important than anything else. Be on guard at all times and avoid the Demas Syndrome.

Counterfeit Cravings

The third thing that can choke the growth of the Word of God is the lust we have for the things of this world. It is a counterfeit craving because it blinds us to what is truly important.

Dave Roper gives a good definition of worldliness. "Worldliness is reading magazines about people who live hedonistic lives and spend too much money on themselves and wanting to be like them. But more importantly, worldliness is simply pride and selfishness in disguise."[2]

Riches are like a beautiful oasis that we see far off in the desert. Because we see water ahead, we drink all of our reserve. As we stagger forward we discover that what we thought was a placid pond is really scorching sand. That is the deceitfulness of riches. They entice us with thoughts of grandeur and power; but when we actually see them through the eyes of our Lord, we see that they are meant to be used for the good of others, not ourselves. There is nothing wrong with wealth, as long as wealth doesn't choke our Christian lives.

I have seen Christians who use their resources for the Lord. Whenever there has been a need, they were quick to volunteer their time and personal money to help out. But there are other Christians to whom riches matter far too much. The actual economic status of these Christians doesn't seem to matter. They can be rich or poor. But they have let their own lust for money run rampant to the point that it has consumed and ruined their Christian lives.

I had some friends who were multimillionaires. They hit a chicken while driving. They stopped the car, picked up the chicken and took it to the gas station to trade it for gasoline. These people also worried constantly that they would not have enough money to pay their taxes. This is an example of people whose effectiveness for Christ was ruined by their craving for worldly possessions.

I have found that it is sometimes easier to witness to those who have "made it" financially rather than the "up-and-comers." The up-and-comers seem to have no time to listen to me because they are on their way up the corporate ladder and they are afraid to stop for even a minute. They are consumed by their counterfeit, worldly cravings. The ones who have made it, sometimes realize the futility of what they have accomplished and are eager to learn more about Christ.

Dear friend, I challenge you to analyze your own life. Are you using your money wisely for the work of the Kingdom? Or are you squandering it down on this earth? Decide today to keep the Big Three—the creeping cares, the sham of worldly success, and counterfeit cravings—from disabling your walk with Christ.

The Living Word
And these are they which are sown among thorns; such as hear the word. And the cares of this world, and the deceitfulness of riches, and the lusts of other things entering in, choke the word, and it becometh unfruitful. Mark 4:18–19

God has great regard for His Word. We should treat it with high regard and apply it to every part of our lives. I know that there are many people who listen to me preach who feel convicted immediately after the service. Perhaps they realize that the desire to keep up with the Joneses is ruining their walk with Christ. But the conviction doesn't last. They might feel inspired all the way to the car and even as they pull out of the parking lot. But after they arrive at work the next morning, they forget the warning.

Seeing a co-worker's new suit puts them in a covetous frame of mind once again.

We need to be careful to let the Word of God permeate every part of our lives. We need to understand the high regard that God has for His Word.

Take a minute and think about what the Word of God means to you. Do you feel the presence of God in your life? Are you letting the Word of God get choked out by the Big Three? Don't let your life get wrapped up in the now. Instead, focus on the eternal. Plan each day for every part of your life to glorify God.

Powerful Prayer

When researchers with the Gallup organization surveyed Americans regarding the role of prayer in their lives, they discovered that 82% of the female respondents said prayer was important, while 69% of the men said it was important.[3] But while a pretty high percentage of people say prayer is important to them, there isn't much evidence that they believe what they say. Dallas Willard must have observed the same thing. He said, "The 'open secret' of many 'Bible-believing' churches is that a vanishing small percentage of those talking about prayer… are actually doing what they are talking about."[4]

Developing a strong prayer life is of crucial importance in our Christian lives. When we learn to pray to our Heavenly Father, we will learn how to stay strong in our Christian lives. The cares of the world will be less likely to make an impression on us. The delusion of wealth won't have the same impact on our souls. The constant yearning for things other than the things of God will diminish.

When is the right time to pray? First, pray constantly (Luke 18:1; 1 Thessalonians 5:17). While you should have a daily quiet time of prayer with the Lord (Luke 11:3), you should also talk to your Heavenly Father throughout the day as you would with a close friend. You need to be in a constant state of prayer, always ready to talk to the Lord about every need. Learn to pray every time you sin (1 John 1:9). Ask His forgiveness for the sin you have committed. You will then restore delightful fellowship with your Heavenly Father.

What are some key elements to prayer? The first is to pray believing (Matthew 21:22, Mark 9:23). Pray in God's will. Don't ask for things that God wouldn't want us to have (John 14:13). Finally, pray insistently (Luke 18:1–7). Don't stop praying just because it seems like God hasn't answered our prayer. Trust His will and His way, though it may take time for God to show us what He wants.

Dr. Helen Roseveare, missionary to Zaire, said, "A mother at our mission station died after giving birth to a premature baby. We tried to improvise an incubator to keep the infant alive, but the only hot water bottle we had was beyond repair. So we asked the children to pray for the baby and for her sister. One of the girls responded, 'Dear God, please send a hot water bottle today. Tomorrow will be too late because by then the baby will be dead. And dear Lord, send a doll for the sister so she won't feel so lonely.' That afternoon a large package arrived from England. The children watched eagerly as we opened it. Much to their surprise, under some clothing was a hot water bottle!

Immediately the girl who had prayed so earnestly started to dig deeper, exclaiming, 'If God sent that, I'm sure He also sent a doll!' And she was right! The heavenly Father knew in advance of that child's sincere requests, and five months earlier He had led a ladies' group to include both of those specific articles."

Spend time learning the discipline of prayer. You will find a well of constant strength and encouragement that will help keep the cares of the world at bay.

Craving the Consecrated
Paul explains, *For to be carnally minded is death; but to be spiritually minded is life and peace.* Romans 8:6. The word "carnal"

means "fleshly or worldly." When we center our thoughts and actions on the things of this world, we will stop being effective for the Kingdom of God. We will let the Big Three choke our growth.

How can we stay spiritually minded then? By building up our spiritual nature, learning the principles of God, and applying these truths to our lives. Romans 12:2 states, *And be not conformed to this world: but be ye transformed by the renewing of your mind, that ye may prove what is that good, and acceptable, and perfect, will of God.*

Another verse that can help us is 2 Corinthians 6:17, *Wherefore come out from among them, and be ye separate, saith the Lord, and touch not the unclean thing; and I will receive you.*

Ephesians 5:11 says, *And have no fellowship with the unfruitful works of darkness, but rather reprove them.*

John Mason Brown was a drama critic and speaker well known for his witty and informative lectures on theatrical topics. One of his first important appearances as a lecturer was at the Metropolitan Museum of Art. Brown was pleased, but also rather nervous, and his nerves were not helped when he noticed by the light of the slide projector that someone was copying his every gesture. After a time he broke off his lecture and announced with great dignity that if anyone was not enjoying the talk, he was free to leave. Nobody did, and the mimicking continued. It was another 10 minutes before Brown realized that the mimic was his own shadow!

Was Brown's shadow real? Of course. Does a shadow have the power to control a person's actions? Of course not. It can only mimic. But in Brown's case, his shadow did take control momentarily. Why? Because he allowed himself to be so distracted — "addicted," if you will — by it that he completely forgot what he was supposed to be doing. That's a pretty good description of the sin nature we carry within us as redeemed people. It can cause havoc, even though it has been made powerless by our identification with Christ.[5]

Don't let the "shadow" of your flesh control you. Instead, open yourself up to the Word of God. Stay away from a covetous attitude. Put a lock on your old nature. Pour pesticide on those nasty habits. Instead learn to spend your day in an attitude of prayer. You will find that prayer is the Miracle-Gro of growth and the secret to continued progress and power!

-5-

Your Harvest Awaits

God is ready to assume full responsibility
for the life wholly yielded to Him.
~Andrew Murray~

Every Wednesday afternoon, I check in on the church kitchen to see how everything is going. Jon Laegeler, who runs this huge operation, is always in motion. He stops only to give me a report. Jon supervises and cooks over 500 meals a day. All of our pre-schoolers, kindergarteners, grade-schoolers, middle-schoolers, high-schoolers, and staff eat nutritious lunches.

In addition to this, on Wednesdays the kitchen staff prepares 100–200 pizzas and other short-order items for dinner. Church members and school parents can order a pizza to go and eat it at home with their families before coming back to church for the evening service, or they may just stay and eat in our church cafeteria.

I enjoy watching Jon add the yeast to the bowl for the pizza dough. He usually adds about four ounces of yeast to make 100 12-inch pizzas. It always seems like such a little bit of yeast to make that much dough. When I come back a few hours later, there is always a mountain of dough waiting to be formed into pizza crusts.

It is easy to compare what Jon does week after week to the Christian life. There are a lot of ingredients necessary to help a Christian grow—Bible study, prayer, church attendance, fellowship, and witnessing are just a few of these components. When you mix in the yeast of the Holy Spirit, the ingredients form a wonderfully productive Christian.

Jesus explained this principle in His final episode from the parable of the sower. He shows us what happens when the seed of the Word falls on good ground.

And other fell on good ground, and did yield fruit that sprang up and increased; and brought forth, some thirty, and some sixty, and some an hundred. Mark 4:8

And these are they which are sown on good ground; such as hear the word, and receive it, and bring forth fruit, some thirtyfold, some sixty, and some an hundred. Mark 4:20

We have studied many different types of people in this parable. We first looked at what happened when the seed fell on the wayside and Satan snatched it away before the person could trust Christ. We saw that some of the seed fell in shallow ground; and when the persecution came, the seed couldn't produce. Then we saw that creeping cares, the sham of worldly success, and covetousness can choke the seed's production.

But now something exciting has happened. The seed has fallen on the good ground. The results are sure, and a great harvest is guaranteed. Fasten your seatbelts, folks; this person is going to produce!

How to Get Results

Think for a moment about the differences between the shallow ground, the weedy ground, and the good ground. The shallow ground has rocks just below the surface. A thin layer of good soil is on top of the rock, so when the seed is sown it germinates, but is unable to form strong roots. How would a farmer make shallow soil into good soil? First, he would have to remove the rocks. It might take some time, but the end result of soft, fertile ground would make the harvest possible.

When the seed is sown, careful maintenance is required if the seeds will grow up free of the choking weeds.

It also takes daily surveillance of the ground to make sure weeds don't grow. A couple in Arkansas had their garden in a dry riverbed where the soil was particularly rich. Anything they planted grew, but so did the weeds. There were a few weeks when the husband hadn't had the time to check out the garden. When he finally walked by, he saw the weeds were taller than he was!

The good soil is only good because it doesn't have rocks impeding the seed from taking root and because the weeds are continually pulled. It is the same in our Christian lives. In order to produce 30-fold, 60-fold, or even 100-fold, the soil of our lives needs continual work.

Angie was the kind of person who always had a lot of friends. She made friends easily and enjoyed hanging out with them at parties and bars. After she trusted Christ, she witnessed to her friends, but they laughed at her. The next time she wanted to go shopping, she asked her friend, Ashley, to accompany her. Ashley mumbled some excuse, acting like she wanted to get off the phone. A week or two later, she asked Ashley to go somewhere with her again. Instead, Ashley invited Angie to a party she was going to that night.

Angie hesitated. She had started to read her Bible and realized that her old life wasn't pleasing to God, but she still wanted to be with her friends, so she reluctantly said she would go.

As she got ready to go to the party, she felt bad inside, like she was doing something wrong. She knew there would be drinking and her friends would start acting really stupid. Just before she left, Faye, one of her new friends from church, called asking Angie to go and help her with the church's soup kitchen. Angie quickly agreed, her heart feeling lighter than it had felt all week. She called Ashley back and told her that she couldn't go to the party after all. Ashley didn't act that disappointed, and Angie realized that her friends probably didn't want her around because she had changed so much. As she helped Faye dish out food, she understood that her new way of life would involve some choices about her friends.

When Angie made that important decision, she was working on the soil of her heart. She was breaking up a layer of rock and hoeing some creeping "weedy" sins. Now the Holy Spirit can work with the sown Word of God, making Angie into a productive, profitable Christian.

Let Go So You Can Grow

The word "yield" in the Greek is *didome,* and means "to bring forth; to deliver; to grant; to give; to make; or to have power." If we put God's Word into our minds, it will generate thirty-, sixty-, or one hundred-fold. It is exciting to note the yield begins at thirty-fold. If the Word of God is working in our lives, we are guaranteed at least thirty-fold.

The word "sprang" in the Greek is *anabaino,* which means "to ascend; to climb; to grow; or to come up." In other words, if we are doing the right things in the Christian life, God gives the blessing and the increase!

Every farmer knows that it takes a lot of work to maintain a garden. As I've mentioned before, the soil needs to be worked before the seed can be planted. The weeds need to be tended so that the tender plants aren't choked out. But if it doesn't rain, then the field won't produce, either. In the end, even with the farmer doing everything right, he is dependent on God to send rain.

It is the same way with the Christian life. If we don't prepare the soil of our own hearts, then the Word of God won't be able to sink deep roots. If we don't resist temptation, then we won't grow as you should. When we have done all that we can do, we need to let go so we can grow. God will handle the actual growing process in our lives.

So take a moment right now and consider the soil of your own heart. Have you prepared it by breaking up any "rocks" below the surface that will impede your growth? Are you constantly monitoring what kind of things enter your mind — like television shows and movies that fail to glorify God? Do you watch out for the weeds of gossip and criticism? Are you reading the Word of God daily and attending church regularly in order to get as much of the "seed" as you can? Then you can expect growth! God will use you for His work; you can be assured of that.

Two Tips
The Word of God is more than an intellectual entity. We can't put a timer on how God will produce growth in our lives. We can't study for 30 hours in order to produce 30-fold, 60 hours for 60-fold, 100 hours for 100-fold. These verses of Scripture aren't meant as an exact equation. God uses different people in different ways. Whether the harvest is 30-, 60-, or 100-fold is up to Him.

Here are two tips that will help us experience spiritual victory. The first is *Patience*. I'm reminded of the old story about the man who prayed for patience and said, "Lord, I want it now!" We all tend to want instant growth. Just as a mighty oak takes many years to produce shade, so it takes time for God's Word to mature us into God's wonderful workmanship. We tend toward impatience. We expect the seed of the Word of God to grow like the stalk did in "Jack and the Beanstalk."

Amy Carmichael, the great missionary to India, wrote some great words on this subject. She said,

> Sometimes when we read the words of those who have been more than conquerors, we feel almost despondent. I feel that I shall never be like that. But they won through step by step, by little bits of wills, little denials of self, little inward victories,

by faithfulness in very little things. They became what they are. No one sees these little, hidden steps. They only see the accomplishment; but even so, those small steps were taken. There is no sudden triumph, no sudden spiritual maturity. That is the work of the moment"[1]

Isaiah 28:10 says, *For precept must be upon precept, precept upon precept; line upon line, line upon line; here a little and there a little:*

Galatians 6:9 states, *And let us not be weary in well doing: for in due season we shall reap, if we faint not.*

If anybody had ever told me that I was going to study the Bible as my lifework, I would have said, "NEVER, it's too boring!" Then I accepted Christ and started living for Him. The Bible became the most exciting book I had ever known. There is NO book comparable to it!

Having patience is difficult. Most people don't like waiting for anything very long; they want everything at their convenience. In Israel, they needed the early *and* the latter rains. They had to be patient, though, as they waited for both rains; these rains guaranteed a great crop.

On a past trip to the Holy Land, we encountered many days of rainy weather. That particular year, Israel had more rain and snow than any other time in recorded history. The Sea of Galilee and the Jordan River were overflowing their banks. The Israelis didn't have to be patient for the rain to come; they had to be patient for the rain to stop!

Incidentally, we took a trip several years later, and Israel was encountering the opposite problem. That whole region was experiencing a severe drought. The Sea of Galilee was receding terribly and the Jordan River was reduced to a mere stream.

Our lives will produce fruit, if we have patience. There will be times of overflowing blessings, and there will be times of spiritual drought. But in feast *and* famine, we must have patience that God is working His perfect will.

Attention!

The second tip is *Pay Attention*. Be aware of continued opportunities to grow. If you are already attending church regularly, then perhaps it is time for you to volunteer to help out around the church. If you read your Bible for a few minutes every day, then why don't you set aside part of your lunch hour each day to get in some additional "spiritual exercise." Don't miss an opportunity that God is giving you to grow.

Gordon was a Christian for quite a few years before any measurable growth took place in his life. He was happy to attend church when it was convenient. He even dusted off his Bible occasionally. But one day after he had attended a special India outreach meeting, he wrote out a check and told me he hoped that it would be a help to those who needed it. Gordon and I started talking; and he told me about his wife, Janna. She wasn't a Christian and had no desire to attend church with her husband. Gordon told me how he personally hadn't grown too much in his Christian life. But he shared that now he felt convicted to open himself up to as many opportunities for growth as possible.

Not long after that, I saw Gordon in the front of our church pulling weeds out of our flowerbeds. I told him that I appreciated his efforts. He told me that his wife had been so impressed that he was willing to do work for the church that she had gone out and bought a whole bunch of flowers for him to add to the beds. A few weeks later, I saw Janna outside helping Gordon. Apparently she loved gardening.

It took about six more months; but one day Janna, came to church. Two months after that, she trusted Christ as her Savior. Somehow

Gordon's act of service opened his wife's eyes to the truth. She realized that Gordon had something she didn't have.

Gordon was fortunate that he chose to pay attention to opportunities for growth. We need to do the same. We need to stay aware of chances to strengthen our faith.

You may be asking, "What do I actually do to produce 30-, 60-, or 100-fold?" I believe everybody can produce fruit, no matter what their abilities or shortcomings. But the key is, we need to take advantage of opportunities to grow spiritually. Our local church could always use volunteer labor. A teenager down the street might appreciate some one-on-one time. A neighbor girl might enjoy coming to the youth program at church. Whatever the opportunity is, take it! You'll be surprised at how much you'll grow.

No Excuses

Remember, God gave us our abilities and talents in the first place. He wants us to use those talents for His service, no matter how meager they might seem. Some may start out with just one talent; others may start out with one hundred talents. I don't believe there is a Christian in the world that can't produce 30-, 60-, or 100-fold. Every Christian can experience fruit in their lives because bearing fruit comes through faithful obedience to God. Not everybody can sing and not everybody can be a preacher, but every Christian can be faithful and submissive.

Ralph Kowalski was a man that some people might look at and say, "How could God use him?" He was born with some problems; and consequently, had mild seizures throughout the day. Small in stature, he sometimes accidentally spit on people he was talking to. I first met him when Linda and I started in the city of Chicago. Somehow he had heard of me, and he knew the name of the street where our church was meeting. He walked along the street knocking on every door until finally he came to our small storefront. We struck up an instant friendship, and he became one of our first members.

Ralph didn't let his physical infirmities stop him from using the opportunities he was given to serve. He was one of the greatest soul-winners I knew. One day I got a call from Ralph. He was working as a janitor at a public school. He was witnessing to a teacher there and called me to come help him lead the teacher to Christ. I drove to the school and found the teacher ready to trust Christ as his Savior.

Years ago, Ralph suffered a fatal heart attack. I will always have a special place in my heart for this great man of God. He didn't let anything stop him from growing. I know a lot of people with many more talents and abilities than Ralph had, but they complain that they don't have enough ability to be used of God. Ralph knew what some people don't: God can use anyone. The key is in our willingness to obey the call of God upon our lives.

Fabulous Fruit

My son, Jim, and his wife Karen, took their children, Amy and Erica, apple-picking when the girls were younger. The girls both held onto either handle of the bushel basket as they eagerly walked into the orchard.

"I'm going to get the most apples," Erica said with a smile.

"Oh yeah?" Amy teased, "Try and beat me!"

The two girls picked as many apples as they could reach. Then Amy spied the perfect apple.

"Daddy, do you see that apple? Would you mind getting it for me? It is too high for me to reach."

Jim will do anything for his girls. He climbed a ladder that was already in the tree and reached as high as he could. His fingers closed around the apple and he handed it down to Amy.

"Thanks, Daddy," Amy said as she took a huge bite, "This one tastes the best!"

What if my son's family went to the apple orchard at the right time of year but found no apples? "Sorry," the orchard management would say, "We didn't have a harvest this year. None of the trees produced any fruit."

Amy and Erica wouldn't have liked that very much, and neither would I.

It is essential that we produce fruit in our Christian lives. A fruitful Christian is a happy Christian. Read the following verse. It talks about the fruit we should produce.

But the fruit of the Spirit is love, joy, peace, longsuffering, gentleness, goodness, faith, Meekness, temperance: against such there is no law. Galatians 5:22–23

When the Christian grows in Christ, they will be more loving, more joyful, more peaceful, more longsuffering, and more gentle. As they mature and change, these characteristics will describe their life. And remember, we don't have to have only one kind of fruit in our life. Unlike the apple tree that can only produce apples, the Christian can and should produce every one of the Fruits of the Spirit.

Another fruit that we should have in our lives is souls. Proverbs 11:30 states, *The fruit of the righteous is a tree of life; and he that winneth souls is wise.* When we take every opportunity to share our faith, then we will be rewarded with the wonderful fruit of souls won for Christ.

When I attended Bible college, there was a group of us who studied and learned together. We loved to witness and talk to each other about the people we were witnessing to. One day I was out walking on Miami Beach passing out Heaven tracts, when I came across a Catholic priest. I didn't know he was a priest at first. I had the privilege of leading him to Christ. He invited my friends and I to the Catholic school where he taught. He invited us to talk to each class. It was a once-in-a-lifetime opportunity. I spent time explaining the gospel and then asked the students to accept Christ. After an hour or so, the officials of the school came and politely asked us to leave, but many souls were won before we had to go.

Sometimes we will have these kinds of opportunities to witness. Don't pass them by! Other times we can witness one-on-one. Whatever the setting, don't ever pass by an opportunity to experience the fruit of witnessing.

A Yankee soldier on sentry duty was standing at the gateway of the Northern army. The soldier said, "Stop!" as a man came galloping up on a horse. He took his gun and held it to the man's chest and shouted, "I have been ordered to shoot and kill anybody that does not know the password! What is the password?"

The man on the horse replied, "Lincoln."

The soldier said, "Wrong. That's not the password." Somehow the man had forgotten the password. He continued, "If I didn't know you, I would blow you off that horse right now. But I remember you and know you are a loyal soldier. Go back and get the password."

The man went back and then returned with the password. With a sincere thank you, he said, "You have just saved my life; now I want to share something with you that will save yours. Jesus shed His blood on the cross of Calvary almost 2,000 years ago so that we can have eternal life simply by believing in that payment for our sins."

The Yankee soldier looked at him and said, "I also have been born again in the blood of the Lord Jesus Christ. I know that salvation is not by works of righteousness that we've done. A Sunday School teacher back in Pennsylvania many years ago taught this to me."

That Sunday School teacher had sown a seed many years before, and now the fruit had come by the Yankee soldier giving another person grace. We can experience the fruit of growth in our own lives as well. We can be fabulous fruit-bearing Christians by preparing the soil, having patience, and paying attention to growth. This is why it takes *more* than a miracle to make a Christian grow. First, we must prepare the soil of our own hearts for growth. We must open ourselves to the Word of God and its truths as often as possible. We must work to weed out the sins that can choke out our growth. Then we must be patient as we wait for God's harvest in our lives.

READY, SET, GROW

If God is your copilot, change seats!

Mom and Dad decided to perform an experiment. Mom had complained that the kids weren't listening to her. She told Johnny ten times to clean his room, but he hadn't listened. Telling Jordan to put the dishes in the dishwasher resulted in dirty dishes that still sat on the counter.

The parents checked to make sure the children were in the next room. Then Dad said in a conversational tone to Mom, "I wish Johnny would clean his room." The two waited for a moment, and then Dad continued, "I hope Jordan decides to take care of the dishes." There was still no response from the children. Then Dad said, "I can't wait to eat ice cream after dinner."

Both children immediately bounded into the kitchen. "We heard you!" they shouted.

Johnny and Jordan have a sickness most children have called "selective hearing." They hear what they want to hear and block out the unpleasant.

Jesus ended His parable with an important thought, one we don't want to miss. He knew the tendency people would have to hear words of instruction but then forget about it in their daily walk.

Mark 4:9 states, *And he said unto them, He that hath ears to hear, let him hear.* He was saying, "Don't forget my words. Remember them as you go about your daily lives."

Are you coming down with the debilitating illness called Christian Selective Hearing? Do you listen to a pastor's sermon, and then the next day "forget" to apply that message to your life?

Marianne had this problem during a difficult time at work. Her company was downsizing and everyone was nervous about keeping their positions. Marianne's boss had just been placed in a different part of the organization, and Marianne was sure her job would be reviewed next. Her mind was so caught up in her worries that every time she opened her Bible, she found it hard to read even a few verses. Instead of praying and letting God take care of her problems, she worried about her troubles.

The following Sunday it seemed like Pastor Smith tailored his message especially for her. He spoke on worry and how we should be anxious for nothing. He explained that the answer to worry was prayer. Marianne felt convicted by what the pastor said. She decided to stop letting worry ruin her spiritual walk.

However, when Marianne walked into the office the next day, she knew something was wrong. Everyone was bent over their desks, outwardly working hard. Lately little work had been accomplished because everyone spent most of their time gossiping about what was going to happen to their jobs. As she slid into her chair, she saw that the supervisor for their whole division stood in the corner talking to her team leader. She then understood why no one was talking. She didn't feel like talking, either. She stared at the pile of papers on her desk as she felt worry sicken her mind. When the supervisor left, everyone went back to their normal chatter. Marianne continued to worry throughout the day, forgetting to pray even once.

That Wednesday night, Pastor Smith spoke on selective hearing. He said that when a person feels convicted to change something in his or her life because of something a pastor said or something read from Scripture and they don't change, then that person will never experience victory in their Christian life.

These words made Marianne realize she had done exactly what the pastor had said. On Sunday, she had determined that prayer would be her response to worry, but Monday she was a forgetful hearer.

Do you need to take a moment and determine to let the Word of God saturate every part of your life? Are you like Marianne, tending toward selective hearing? Then remember Jesus' words as He finished the parable of the sower with the warning, "hear my words." Let His words help you and nourish you as you continue to grow spiritually.

The How-To's of Hearing

A preacher that I heard recently said that everyone could learn Scripture. He explained that for some people, this process can take a little longer than others. His wife could look at two verses and memorize them in two or three minutes, but it took him about an hour to learn them. Then he shared that his wife wouldn't remember those verses the next day, but he could remember them for the next twenty years.

That story shows that it doesn't matter what kind of education you have when it comes to God's Word. Scripture is deep enough for the most learned men. Every time the Bible is studied, we will find fresh insight because that is its nature. To the less-learned, the study of the Bible still brings help and peace for the perplexities of the day.

So, don't use the excuse that you don't have enough education to study Scripture. You can and should study, even if you can only absorb one or two verses at once! Here are some of the things you can do with one verse of Scripture. Following these suggestions will help you to apply this verse to your daily life, thereby producing spiritual fruit.

1. Hear it. Romans 10:17 states, *So then faith cometh by hearing, and hearing by the word of God.*

2. Read it. Acts 17:11 says, *These were more noble than those in Thessalonica, in that they received the word with all readiness of mind, and searched the scriptures daily, whether those things were so.*

3. Study it. 2 Timothy 2:15 explains, *Study to shew thyself approved unto God, a workman that needeth not to be ashamed, rightly dividing the word of truth.*

4. Memorize it. Psalm 119:11 says, *Thy word have I hid in mine heart, that I might not sin against thee.*

5. Meditate on it. Joshua 1:8 states, *This book of the law shall not depart out of thy mouth; but thou shalt meditate therein day and night, that thou mayest observe to do according to all that is written therein: for then thou shalt make thy way prosperous, and then thou shalt have good success.*

Getting the Most Out of a Sermon

The clock is ticking down. The crowd is on the edge of their seats. Only a few seconds are left in the basketball game, and one team gets a foul. The referee signals two free throws for the fouled player. As he stands on the free throw line, you notice the tension in the player's face. He knows that it is important that he makes this point.

That player is probably paying more attention to his shooting than he has the entire game. He knows it is important that he makes the shot. This is the same attitude we should have when we listen to a preacher preach the Bible. We need to pay close attention so that the Word can make a difference in our lives.

There's a story about a motel owner who never attended church, but one Sunday, he decided to go. The preacher happened to be preaching on this same parable and said, "He that hath ears, let him hear." The man then childishly put his fingers in his ears.

About that time, a deer fly came and bit him right on the ear. Right as he yanked his fingers out to kill the deer fly, the preacher said again, "He that has ears, let him hear." The motel owner decided he had better listen, and then trusted in Christ. The Lord has a sense of humor, doesn't He?

When you go to church, make sure you keep the preacher tuned in. Don't let an anticipated sporting event keep you from concentrating on what is being said. Don't think about your "to-do" list. Instead, concentrate on the Word of God. This will help you continue well on your spiritual quest.

Here are practical suggestions on getting the most out of a sermon.

1. Prepare to receive the Word. We have studied how we need to prepare the soil of our hearts in order for the seed of the Word of God to flourish, and this principle applies to church as well. Don't plan any big events on Saturday night. Instead, plan for church the next day. If you have children, lay out their clothes. Decide what you are going to wear. If you have to iron a shirt, do it then, not five minutes before you walk out the door on Sunday morning! Start a new tradition in your household. Buy something easy for breakfast the next morning. Maybe a special coffee cake or doughnuts will help make the following morning easier because everyone gets their own breakfast.

2. Give yourself plenty of time to get to church. Get up early enough so that everyone isn't in a bad mood as they rush out the door.

3. Bring your Bible, a notebook, and a pen to church. Not only will this help you get more out of the sermon, but taking notes during the preaching can give you a reference that will help you throughout the week.

4. During the opening hymns, pray that God will prepare your own heart to receive the Word.

5. Use the sermon throughout the week. Don't just absorb all that knowledge without giving some of it away to others! Use the opportunities God gives you to apply what you have learned.

Powerful Word

What does the Word of God mean to you? Hebrews 4:12 says, *For the word of God is quick, and powerful, and sharper than any twoedged sword, piercing even to the dividing asunder of soul and spirit, and of the joints and marrow, and is a discerner of the thoughts and intents of the heart.*

Do you think of the Word of God like a two-edged sword or a knife that couldn't cut hot butter? The Word of God should extend to all our thoughts and actions. It should remain our Compass in a lost world.

James 1:22–25 explains this further. *But be ye doers of the word, and not hearers only, deceiving your own selves. For if any be a hearer of the word, and not a doer, he is like unto a man beholding his natural face in a glass: For he beholdeth himself, and goeth his way, and straightway forgetteth what manner of man he was. But whoso looketh into the perfect law of liberty, and continueth therein, he being not a forgetful hearer, but a doer of the work, this man shall be blessed in his deed.*

As a preacher, I have preached to all kinds of hearers. Some of them I call, "The Perfect Blank Starers"; they don't seem to even know I am preaching. Then there are hearers who simply go to sleep! It reminds me of when I was in Bible college. A friend would always fall asleep during class. It was particularly embarrassing when he would start snoring.

One day in the middle of class, he fell sound asleep. I decided to play a little trick on him. I shook him and said, "The president just called on you to pray." My friend stood right up and started praying. Fortunately, he didn't get in trouble!

Then there are hearers with criticizing ears; they disapprove of what they hear. They seem to enjoy finding fault with a preacher's heartfelt sermons. This is really because they feel convicted from the sermon, but would rather not change whatever sin is a problem in their lives. It is easier for them to criticize than to change.

Others are suspicious hearers; they are apprehensive of everything and everybody. They feel that the only trustworthy person they've ever known is themselves. They look for any opportunity to catch a mistake; and when that blunder comes, WATCH OUT! Their own life may be full of mistakes, yet they only see the faults in others.

Recently, we went to a restaurant that has a great reputation for their Reuben sandwiches. I ordered one, but was disappointed when the sandwich I received had hardly any meat on it. I thought about saying something; but then I thought, "Every time we come here their sandwiches are delicious. I will give them a break." I decided to give them the benefit of the doubt. I didn't want to be a criticizing or suspicious person. Rather I wanted to use the seed of the Word of God to control my reactions.

Do you need to give the benefit of the doubt to your brother or sister in Christ? Perhaps someone has said something that offended you. Perhaps you have criticized someone else without realizing that you are doing the same thing you censured. Take a moment and confess this to God. He will forgive you and help you to have the proper spirit for the next time.

If I don't grow, where do I go?

Aaron was raised in a Christian home. Every night, his mother knelt with him beside his bed and listened to him pray. He trusted Christ at an early age. But at 16, the creeping cares of the world were too much for him. He hung around the wrong people. This continued all through high school and two years of college. One night, he partied with a group of his drinking buddies at one of his friend's homes. Driving home early the next morning, the car was loaded up with his inebriated friends. He never saw the tree until they crashed into it. Somehow everyone survived, though Aaron and the two guys with him in the front seat suffered severe injuries. As Aaron recovered, he suffered intense guilt. He realized his friends could have been killed and it would have been his fault. One day, Aaron scheduled an appointment to talk to me.

Aaron shared with me what had happened and then he said, "Pastor Scudder, do you think I could still be going to Heaven? After what I did, I don't see how God could love me."

I opened my Bible to John 10:28 and read, *I give unto them eternal life; and they shall never perish, neither shall any man pluck them out of my hand.*

"Aaron," I was glad to assure him, "when you trusted Christ, He saved you forever. The payment He made for your sin included all the sins you committed in your past and all the sins you would commit in the future."

I explained to Aaron that the Holy Spirit had sealed him when he trusted Christ. I showed him Ephesians 1:13–14, *In whom ye also trusted, after that ye heard the word of truth, the gospel of your salvation: in whom also after that ye believed, ye were sealed with that holy Spirit of promise, Which is the earnest of our inheritance until the redemption of the purchased possession, unto the praise of his glory.*

I then explained that while a Christian cannot lose their salvation, they can lose their service. Salvation doesn't cost us anything, but discipleship (following Christ) costs everything. Aaron's friends might never go to Heaven because of Aaron's bad testimony in drinking with them. He would still have to suffer the consequences of his actions, but he could be assured of one thing: God would never send him to Hell.

Aaron confessed his sin to God. He claimed 1 John 1:9, *If we confess our sins, he is faithful and just to forgive us our sins, and to cleanse us from all unrighteousness.* He committed his life to serving the Lord and now tries to prepare the soil of his own heart for spiritual growth.

The Parable Unraveled
The disciples listened to Jesus tell the parable of the sower. Later, they took the opportunity to ask Him to tell them more about it. Mark 4:10–12 states, *And when he was alone, they that were about him with the twelve asked of him the parable. And he said unto them, Unto you it is given to know the mystery of the kingdom of God: but unto them that are without, all these things are done in parables: That seeing they may see, and not perceive; and hearing they may hear, and not understand; lest at any time they should be converted, and their sins should be forgiven them.*

Do you remember what a parable is? A parable teaches reality by showing us things in nature and in life. Jesus took a common-sense, everyday occurrence that everybody could identify with and compared it to a truth from the Word of God.

The parable of the sower and the seed is used to show that it takes a certain kind of soil for the Word of God to produce fruit. The Pharisees and others in Christ's time were so involved in trying to find fault with the Savior that they never saw the truth Jesus taught. Jesus' words weren't complex. They weren't hard to understand. He had to "unlearn" the religious multitude of their strife of words and their ceremonies before they could perceive the truth and learn from it. He used examples from the school of nature to help them see the bigger, divine picture.

Jesus made it clear that it was only by the payment that He would make for sin that they could go to Heaven. Jesus taught in parables to give them (and us) the truth about the reason He was on earth. He used everyday stories and illustrations to help them understand His purpose and will. Jesus' heart was to reach those who were lost.

For the Christian, this parable explains how to grow spiritually. For the non-Christian, this parable is to help them see the danger of remaining in the condition they are in.

Your Soil Condition

The seed which is sown is the infallible, inerrant Word of God. The seed is perfect. The Word of God needs to be received into our lives in order for us to go to Heaven. It then takes the right condition of the soil in order for that same seed to produce fruit.

The Word of God has the power to save souls and change lives. There is never any failure or inadequacy on the part of the seed. The seed's ability to produce is only limited by the soil upon which it rests.

The parable reveals four basic kinds of soil. The wayside is the hard-beaten path that rejects God's Word. There are many today in this condition. These people are not going to Heaven because they have discarded God's plan of salvation.

The stony ground is soil that is fertile, but shallow. It receives the seed with enthusiasm, but has no depth to sustain it and the slightest offence will make the plant wither. This represents the person who is saved and who experiences phenomenal growth at first, but then stops growing when they are offended.

The thorny ground is also fertile, but is full of cares and lusts that rob the seed of nourishment. A plant springs up, but is choked and doesn't mature to fruitfulness.

The good soil has prepared for the seed. It is deep, fertile soil, free of weeds. The seed not only springs up, but grows to maturity. This soil ends up with a full-grown Christian, one who stands strong in the difficulties of life.

Remember Jeremiah 4:3? *For this saith the LORD to the men of Judah and Jerusalem, Break up your fallow ground, and sow not among thorns.* Are you prepared to be part of the miracle of Christian growth? Are you going to break up the fallow ground in your life? Are you willing to hoe the rocks of bitterness and resentment, rocks that keep the seed from taking root? Are you going to weed out the choking cares of this world, the sham of worldly success, and your lustful cravings? Will you keep a watch on those things, making sure they don't choke out your Christian growth?

The life of spiritual development is an exciting one, filled with the strong, sure promises of God. Won't you decide right now to be a part of this remarkable miracle, a life of growth?

Notes

Chapter One

1. Dr. Maxwell Maltz, *Bits & Pieces*, June 24, 1993, p. 12.

2. Today in the Word, September 25, 1992.

Chapter Two

1. Wood Kroll, *7 Secrets to Spiritual Success*, (Sisters, OR: Multnomah Publishers, 2000), p. 73.

2. Rob Gilbert, *Bits & Pieces*, September 15, 1994, p. 7–8.

Chapter Four

1. Marco R. Della Cava, usatoday.com, October 4, 2000.

2. Steve Farrar, *Family Survival in the American Jungle*, (Sisters, OR: Multnomah Publishers, 1991) p.68.

3. George Gallup, Jr. and Sarah Jones, *100 Questions and Answers: Religion in America* (Princeton: Princeton Religion Research Center, 1989), p. 39.

4. Wood Kroll, *7 Secrets to Spiritual Success*, (Sisters, OR: Multnomah Publishers, 2000), p. 60.

5. Today in the Word, May 17, 1992.

Chapter Five

1. Tim Hansel, *Holy Sweat*, (Word Books, 1987), p. 130.

Appendix

How to Know for Sure You Are Going to Heaven

Realize first, that everyone is less perfect than a holy God. **We are all sinners and unable to save ourselves.**

For all have sinned, and come short of the glory of God.
Romans 3:23

God says that even our good deeds are unclean in His sight. Our good deeds can never pay the price for our sin.

But we are all as an unclean thing, and all our righteousnesses are as filthy rags; and we all do fade as a leaf; and our iniquities, like the wind, have taken us away. Isaiah 64:6

The result and penalty of sin is death, which means separation from God forever.

For the wages of sin is death; but the gift of God is eternal life through Jesus Christ our Lord. Romans 6:23

Because we have sinned, we all deserve to be separated from God forever. God hates sin because it separates us from Him; but He loves us, the sinners.

Heaven is a perfect place; therefore no sin can enter there. Man must be perfect to gain entrance.

And there shall in no wise enter into it any thing that defileth, neither whatsoever worketh abomination, or maketh a lie: but they which are written in the Lamb's book of life. Revelation 21:27

Nothing man can do could help obtain the perfection God requires for Heaven.

For by grace are ye saved through faith; and that not of yourselves: it is the gift of God: Not of works, lest any man should boast. Ephesians 2:8–9

Salvation is only by God's grace. "Grace" means "unmerited favor or undeserved mercy." A gift is not earned or paid for or it would not be a gift.

But to him that worketh not, but believeth on him that justifieth the ungodly, his faith is counted for righteousness. Romans 4:5

Christ made a complete payment for all sin and offers His righteousness to us.

For he [God] hath made him [Christ] to be sin for us, who knew no sin; that we might be made the righteousness of God in him. 2 Corinthians 5:21

We have seen that we are all sinners and that the penalty of sin is eternal separation from God. We have also seen that God loves us and offers us the gift of eternal life. He requires only our belief, our trust in that payment.

How could a holy God give eternal life to sinners? Only through His Son, who shed His blood on the cross and rose again. His death paid the complete penalty for our sin, and His resurrection shows God accepted that payment.

All we have to do to have eternal life is believe that Jesus Christ died on the cross to pay for all of our sins and rose again.

For God so loved the world, that he gave his only begotten Son, that whosoever believeth in him should not perish, but have ever-lasting life. John 3:16

This verse does not say anything about promising God good works in order to be saved. It doesn't mention joining a church, being baptized, or even quitting all of your sinning. The word "believe" means "to trust, depend, or rely upon."

Will you place your trust in Jesus Christ to save your soul? To trust Him means to rely totally on Him, not on your own good works. Will you do this right now?

If you have trusted Jesus Christ as your Savior, then you can know you have eternal life. **God has promised this in His Word.**

These things have I written unto you that believe on the name of the Son of God; that ye may <u>know</u> that ye have eternal life, and that ye may believe on the name of the Son of God. 1 John 5:13

For more information and resources contact:
InGrace Ministries
24126 N. Quentin Road
Lake Zurich, IL 60047
800-784-7223
ingrace.us

About Dr. James A. Scudder

Dr. James A. Scudder, the son of a Methodist preacher, was born in Kentucky on July 6, 1946. After graduating from Florida Bible College in 1971, he and his wife Linda and their two small children, Julie and James Jr., immediately left to start a church in Chicago. The Quentin Road Baptist Church began in a storefront on Fullerton Avenue and is now located on 45 acres in Lake Zurich, Illinois. During this time, he also founded one of the nation's largest Christian preschools, a private Christian school for grades K–12th, and Dayspring Bible College & Seminary. Dr. Scudder authored over 12 books and for many years hosted the television and radio broadcast *Victory In Grace*. On September 18, 2016, he retired after 45 faithful years in ministry and passed his thriving ministry on to his son, Jim. On March 24, 2020, Dr. Scudder went home to Glory. There is no doubt, he has received his "Well Done" degree from his Savior.